Bay Shore Park

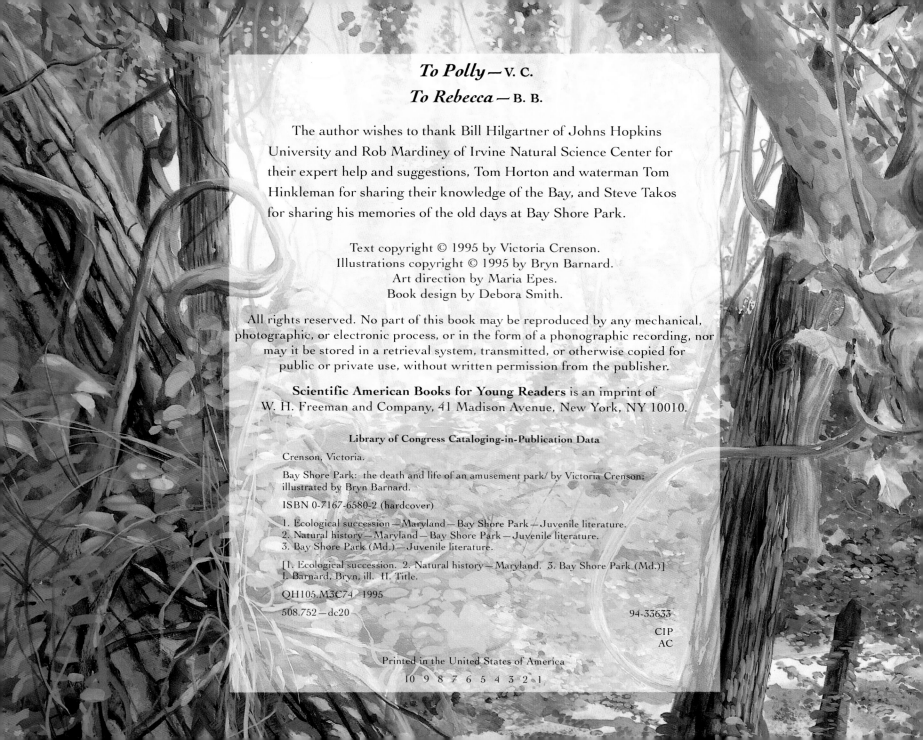

To Polly — V. C.
To Rebecca — B. B.

The author wishes to thank Bill Hilgartner of Johns Hopkins
University and Rob Mardiney of Irvine Natural Science Center for
their expert help and suggestions, Tom Horton and waterman Tom
Hinkleman for sharing their knowledge of the Bay, and Steve Takos
for sharing his memories of the old days at Bay Shore Park.

Text copyright © 1995 by Victoria Crenson.
Illustrations copyright © 1995 by Bryn Barnard.
Art direction by Maria Epes.
Book design by Debora Smith.

Scientific American Books for Young Readers is an imprint of
W. H. Freeman and Company, 41 Madison Avenue, New York, NY 10010.

Library of Congress Cataloging-in-Publication Data

Crenson, Victoria.

Bay Shore Park: the death and life of an amusement park/ by Victoria Crenson;
illustrated by Bryn Barnard.

ISBN 0-7167-6580-2 (hardcover)

1. Ecological succession — Maryland — Bay Shore Park — Juvenile literature.
2. Natural history — Maryland — Bay Shore Park — Juvenile literature.
3. Bay Shore Park (Md.) — Juvenile literature.

[1. Ecological succession. 2. Natural history — Maryland. 3. Bay Shore Park (Md.)]
I. Barnard, Bryn, ill. II. Title.

QH105.M3C74 1995

508.752 — dc20   94-33633
                                                      CIP
                                                      AC

Printed in the United States of America
10 9 8 7 6 5 4 3 2 1

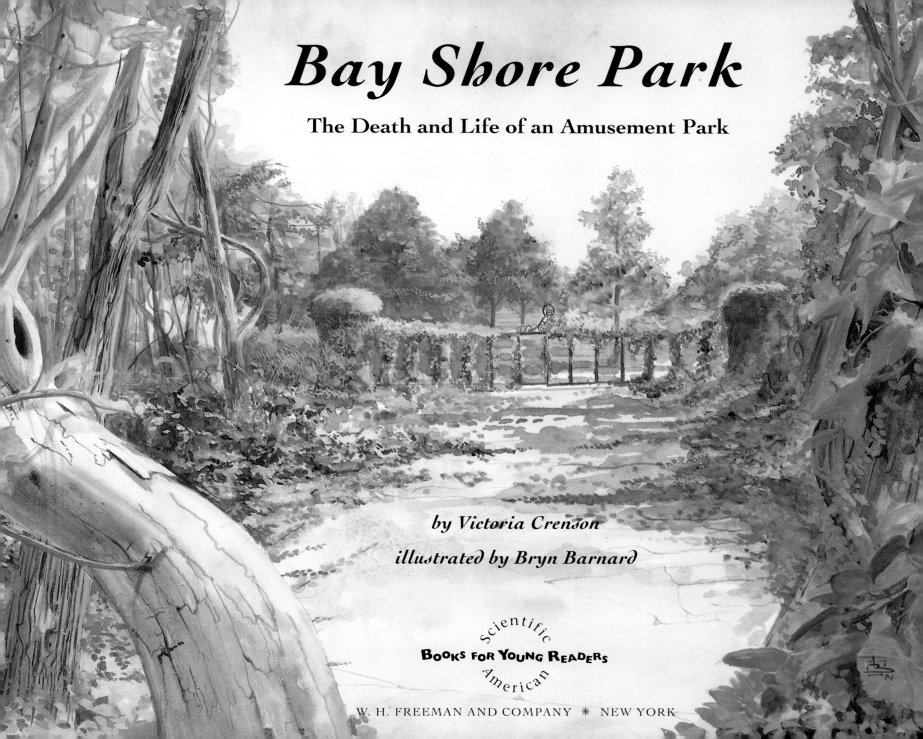

Bay Shore Park

The Death and Life of an Amusement Park

by Victoria Crenson

illustrated by Bryn Barnard

Scientific
BOOKS FOR YOUNG READERS
American

W. H. FREEMAN AND COMPANY ✳ NEW YORK

Summers

1906–1947

Once there was an amusement park on the shore of the upper Chesapeake Bay. For forty-one summers, trolley cars crowded with people from the city of Baltimore clattered and squeaked into the station at Bay Shore Park. The people poured out onto the wide lawns and walkways around the fountain, their arms full of beach blankets and picnic baskets. A cool breeze off the water carried the smells of caramel popcorn, deep-fried crab cakes, suntan lotion, and fresh-cut grass.

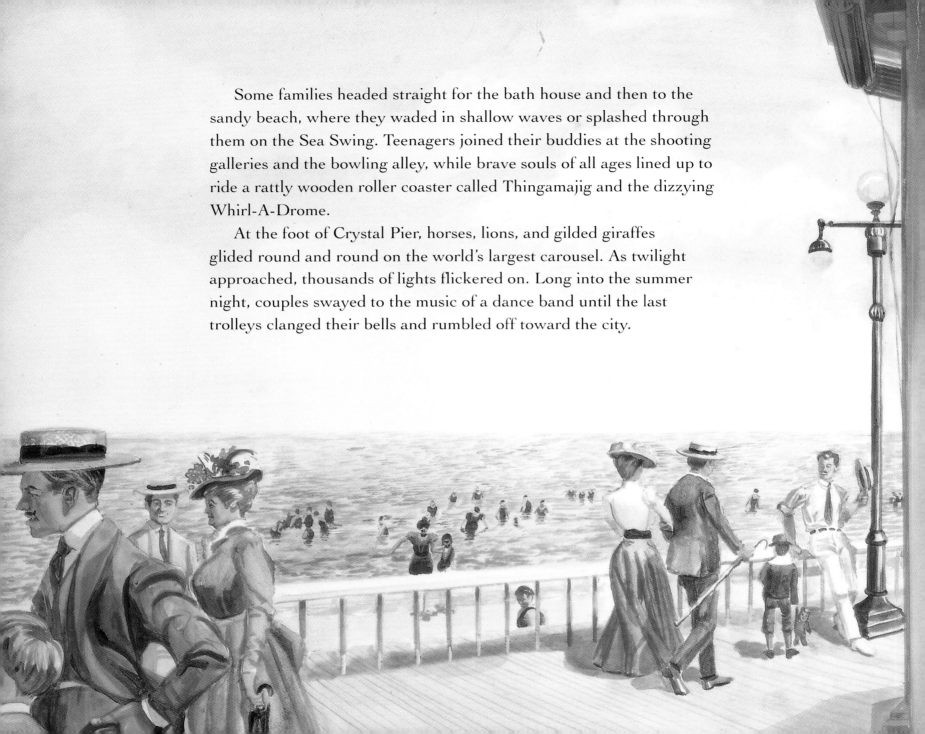

Some families headed straight for the bath house and then to the sandy beach, where they waded in shallow waves or splashed through them on the Sea Swing. Teenagers joined their buddies at the shooting galleries and the bowling alley, while brave souls of all ages lined up to ride a rattly wooden roller coaster called Thingamajig and the dizzying Whirl-A-Drome.

At the foot of Crystal Pier, horses, lions, and gilded giraffes glided round and round on the world's largest carousel. As twilight approached, thousands of lights flickered on. Long into the summer night, couples swayed to the music of a dance band until the last trolleys clanged their bells and rumbled off toward the city.

Every year the park grew bigger. Added attractions clustered around the Crystal Pier and stretched out along a loop of trolley track that skirted the marsh. Year after year the crowds returned.

Then, in the fall of 1947, the park was sold to a giant steel company, whose owners wanted the land for the site of a future factory. The carousel, Thingamajig, the Whirl-A-Drome, the miniature railroad, and all the other rides were taken apart and sold at auction. Bulldozers tore up lawns and demolished buildings, leaving only the trolley station, the fountain, and a generator building standing. In a steady autumn rain, a caravan of dump trucks hauled away debris. The park's great iron entrance gates were padlocked behind them.

Seeds, Weeds, and Pioneers
⟶ Autumn 1947-Spring 1948 ⟵

They come on the Bay breeze, sailing in on downy parachutes. They hitch rides in the mud balls on ducks' feet. They arrive hooked on the feathers of gulls.

Seeds. Zillions of seeds.

Some fall on the concrete walk of the Crystal Pier and are swept away by the wind into the Bay. Others land on bare, muddy earth where the carousel once stood or nestle into cracks and edges of walkways around the fountain. Milkweed, burdock, dandelion, thistle, garlic mustard, bermuda grass, and many others—these are the pioneer invaders. All the while, other seeds that once lay deep and dormant in the soil wait to emerge and take over the newly disturbed ground.

As spring sunshine warms the soil, the first seeds to sprout have an advantage. They thrust down roots to suck up water and minerals, and they push up through the soil to reach sunlight. To find what they need to thrive and spread, early winners in the land-grab use an assortment of survival strategies. A single pigweed plant produces hundreds of thousands of seeds. Bermuda grass stretches out runners, called rhizomes, to create new plants and widen its turf. Other grasses and weeds grow tall quickly and shade out smaller plants.

Two Norway maples that once flanked the steps of the dance pavilion launch their helicopter seeds. The wind carries some of them past the fountain, where they bump against the privet hedge and fall to the ground.

By late summer a lacy carpet of bermuda grass traces cracks in the walkway. Dandelions and spiky plantains have muscled their way through to the full sunlight.

Warfare on the Pier

⟫⟫ Summer 1950 ⟪⟪

At the foot of Crystal Pier tall milkweed, Queen Anne's lace, thistle, and chicory are in bloom. An orange-and-black-striped monarch butterfly unfurls its long proboscis and greedily probes the milkweed's fragrant flowers. The plant uses scent and nectar to attract butterflies, bees, beetles, and ants to its flowers. Each visit dusts the insects with pollen grains that stick to fuzzy backs and legs. The insects carry the pollen to other milkweed flowers where it fertilizes egg cells that grow into parachuting seeds.

To keep hungry insects from devouring its leaves, the milkweed uses a chemical weapon—poisonous juices. Nevertheless, monarch caterpillars munch its leaves, milkweed bugs eat its seeds, and milkweed beetles bore into its stem. These insects have developed a resistance to the milkweed's poison. They even use the poison in their own bodies so that birds and other insects will leave them alone.

Overlapping Territories
❧ Spring 1952 ❧

A mockingbird sings furiously from atop the trolley station one spring evening, declaring his domain. Down below in a clump of nodding foxtail grass, a white-footed mouse shinnies up a grass stem and collects seeds in her mouth. Her shiny eyes catch a movement near the marsh elder bush. It is a blacksnake that slithers past and curls up on the nearby seawall, still warm from the afternoon sun. The mouse stuffs more grass seeds into her mouth, jumps down to the ground, and scurries to her nest under an old crate. She pokes her nose out and sniffs the air.

Suddenly, she smells another white-footed mouse. Baring her teeth, she squeaks a warning and then attacks the intruder and chases him to the border of her territory. Satisfied he is gone, she returns to her seed hunting.

She doesn't see the red fox urinating on a young mulberry tree to mark his hunting territory. His ears stand up as he listens to the tiny rustle of the white-footed mouse passing by. The fox pounces, snapping up the mouse in his jaws. Finished with his meal, the fox trots away while the mockingbird trills on.

Within hours another white-footed mouse has found the seed cache under the old crate and has moved it to her new home among the roots of an old sweetgum tree.

Struggle for Light
⊷ Summer-Fall 1955 ⊷

Where the bowling alley once stood, dried grasses lie flattened, pushed this way and that, like mussed hair. Weaving through them, a red artery of Virginia creeper crosses the ground to a young mulberry tree. Day by day, the growing creeper vine uses small suckers to climb the mulberry's slender trunk, twining around the tree as it reaches for sunlight. By midsummer it has reached the top and spreads itself wide.

Honeysuckle, trumpet creeper, and wild grapevines have climbed the pillars of the trolley station and now enshroud the roof. Bees and hummingbirds feed among the tangle. In the fall when wild grapes ripen, flocks of noisy migrating birds gather on the roof and stuff themselves with the sweet fruit. They leave purple droppings on the pavement around the fountain and roost in the young Norway maple and wild cherry trees that have pushed up through the privet hedge.

Dead Gull and the Recyclers

Spring 1958

A dead gull lies on the sandy soil among the marsh elders. Fidgety yellow jackets dance upon the carcass, pulling off tiny pieces of meat with their mandibles. Meanwhile, a horde of ants crawl under the feathers, doing the same. One by one flies arrive and lay eggs inside the ribcage. Within a day, hundreds of wiggling fly larvas called maggots feast on what remains of the flesh. In a few weeks' time, when the carrion feeders are through and the feathers have all blown away, there is nothing left of the gull but scattered bones, a dried wing, and a beak.

Now the decomposers take over. Worms, tiny insects, bacteria, and funguses that live in the soil digest the remains and break them down into mineral nutrients. Plants such as the marsh elders can absorb these nutrients through their roots and use them to grow.

Old Sweetgum
～ Fall-Winter 1962 ～

The huge sweetgum is nearly a century old this winter. It towers above the younger trees that have taken over the carousel site — other sweetgums, wild cherries, Norway maples, sassafras, mulberries, and even the big crooked sycamore with the piebald bark. Perched on top of the old sweetgum, birds can see over the other treetops all the way to the Bay.

Chickadees peck at the gumballs dangling from its bare branches, trying to shake out tiny seeds.

Sweetgum trees not only produce lots and lots of seeds but they also send out rhizomes that run beneath the ground and then sprout new trees. The sweetgum forest that has marched across the sand-and-cinders parking lot most likely owes its life to Old Sweetgum.

Underwater at the Pier

⚒ 1965 ⚒

At the end of Crystal Pier two black ducks bob on the waves above a sunken barge. For years, winter storms buffeted the wood-and-iron vessel, until one day it sank into the sandy Bay bottom. Now its rusty skeleton is encrusted with mussels and seaweed, an underwater garden where small fish find hiding places and blue crabs scuttle.

Fierce storms have taken their toll on the pier too. The concrete seawall is eroded and cracked in many places. Boulder-size chunks have tumbled into the water. Each wave slurps and gurgles around them into hidden crevices where eels, crabs, and shifting schools of minnows feed. At night, larger fish—perch, catfish, and rockfish—visit the pier to hunt and to feed.

Purple Scat

⟫⟫ Spring 1968 ⟪⟪

On a warm spring night, a raccoon waddles along the water's edge looking for something to eat. Churring softly, he climbs the broken seawall and pokes around the ground for grubs or crickets. His sharp eyes spot a dark-purple mulberry, then another and another. Quickly he stuffs them into his mouth and looks for more. Just then, a slight movement attracts his interest. Always curious and still hungry, the raccoon creeps down the pier to investigate.

Among the bushes several ducks sleep on their grassy nests. The raccoon pauses for a moment in the moonlight. His whiskers twitch as he watches the ducks. One of them stirs, and the raccoon lumbers in, sending the startled ducks off their nests in a panic. He grabs a warm duck egg, cracks it, and noisily sucks up its contents. The ducks charge him and beat him with their strong wings. With the eggshell in his jaws, the raccoon trots back down the pier, away from the quacking commotion, to a quiet place where he can lick the shell clean.

As morning approaches, the raccoon follows the trolley-track bed out toward the marsh. He stops by the old generator building to relieve himself. His purple scat is full of mulberry seeds.

Birds, opossums, foxes, squirrels, and mice eat mulberries too. From the animals' purple droppings, fast-growing mulberry trees have many chances to spread their seeds throughout the park.

Hurricane

⟞ June 21, 1972 ⟝

The ground is already soggy from a week of rain when black clouds race in from the northwest and darken the sky. A gusty wind hisses and then shrieks in the tops of the trees. Splat! Splat! Giant-size raindrops pelt the ground faster and faster. Agnes, the most devastating storm of the century, sweeps across the upper Bay.

Twelve inches of rain falls in a single hour. The rain causes flash floods that wash away bridges and roads. Raging floodwaters snatch houses from their foundations and pick up bicycles, street signs, farm animals, trees, and millions of tons of mud and sewage and send them rushing down the Susquehanna River to the Bay.

For days the water rises until it laps over the Crystal Pier, swirls past Old Sweetgum and soaks the floor of the trolley station. When it finally recedes, it leaves behind a layer of stinky mud and lots of debris. All summer the Bay is the color of coffee with cream.

After Agnes
⊰ 1974 ⊱

The bottom of the Bay still looks like a wet, barren desert. A layer of muck from Hurricane Agnes smothered meadows of underwater grasses where softshell crabs, grass shrimp, and baby fish once found shelter. The grass beds had also provided food for ducks and protected the shoreline from wave erosion. Silt washed down from Pennsylvania has made the already shallow water a foot shallower. The beach is littered with branches, a kitchen cabinet, and part of an outdoor grill.

Agnes also deposited silt in the cracked walkways of the Crystal Pier. Bermuda grass, milkweed, thistles, dandelions, and a host of other plants have taken over the new growing spaces.

Mouthful of Mud
~ 1978 ~

A yellow-and-black wasp with a long sticklike waist—a female mud dauber—tests a puddle's edge with her antennas. She finds a spot where the mud is soft and sticky, bends forward, and scoops up a mouthful of mud in her jaws. With her front legs she pats and shapes the mud into a ball about the size of her head. Carefully, she wraps her front legs around the mud ball to steady it and then takes off, her wings working hard to carry the extra weight, her long back legs trailing behind her.

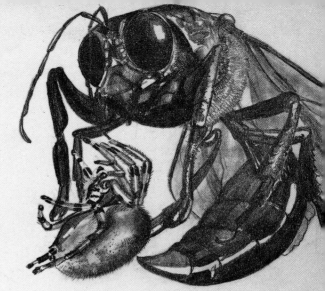

She follows the trolley-track bed as it curves into the woods then peels to the right and shoots through the wide doorway of the generator station. Inside the masonry building it is dark and cool. The once-smooth walls are coated from floor to roof with masses of lumpy mud structures that look like fat macaroni noodles. This mural is the work of many generations of daubers.

The wasp carries the mud ball to the top of a wall. She adds it to a tube she is making, pushing and patting with her jaws and legs. Crawling inside, she smooths the interior walls to finish the tube.

Now the wasp flies back outside. Spying a grass spider, she attacks. She grasps the struggling spider with her legs and uses her stinger to inject a venom that, within seconds, does not kill but paralyzes it. Then she flies to her nest and stuffs the spider deep inside the tube.

More spiders—fifteen in all—she paralyzes and crams inside the mud tube. On the last spider's body she lays a single egg. Then she makes another trip to the shrinking mud puddle and returns with a mud ball to seal off the end of the tube. The egg inside will hatch in a few weeks. The larva will have plenty of fresh meat to eat.

Fountain Forest
~ 1980 ~

The air is heavy and still in the thick forest that has grown up around the fountain. The only sounds are the whirs and buzzes of insects. Grapevines like ancient gnarled arms hang from the trees. Honeysuckle, clematis, and poison ivy reach across the branches and form a nearly closed canopy above, blocking out much of the sunlight. The pavement is blanketed with soil and leaf litter, where shade-loving mosses and mushrooms sprout and poison ivy creeps. Brown sweet-gum balls, Norway maple helicopter seeds, and rotting leaves fill the cement dish of the fountain.

"Tat-tat-tat-tat-tat!" The quiet is interrupted by a redbellied wood-pecker. It hammers again and again at the bark of a dead tree, sending chips of wood flying. By the end of the day, the bird has chiseled a smooth oval entrance to a nesting hole.

Make Way

≈ 1985 ≈

New tenants have arrived to take up residence in the dead tree by the fountain. A family of flying squirrels sleeps together in a furry jumble inside the snug nesting hole. Downstairs, in a cavity among the roots scooped out by a long-departed chipmunk, an old opossum has squeezed in. Opossums are wanderers. This one stays only one day and then moves on. None of the sleeping mammals is bothered by the "tat-tat-tat-tat-tat" of a woodpecker that visits the tree searching for beetle larvas or by the constant comings and goings of honeybees to and from their hive in a hollow branch.

Eagles
1990

There is an enormous messy nest of sticks in the crotch of a tree near the shoreline. Perched above the nest is a large bird with a hooked beak—an eagle. The wind ruffles the white feathers of his head as he scans the Bay. All at once, the eagle is in the air. With a few beats of his great wings he is soaring over the Crystal Pier. He dips one wing, banks to the left, then descends, almost skimming the surface of the water. His talons move forward. In one motion he plucks a squirming fish from the Bay and carries it back to the nest. Together he and his mate tear the fish into pieces small enough for the snapping beaks of their two hungry eaglets.

Old Bay Shore and the nearby marsh have been bought from the steel company as public land. The entrance gate has been opened and people have returned to the park. They watch the eagles through binoculars, talk in excited whispers, and listen to the gentle "frrush-crrush" of waves against the shore.

Old and New

~ 1994 ~

Park workers rip vines from the trolley barn and rebuild its roof.
With chainsaws they cut away the growth around the fountain
and shovel clean its walkways. A parking lot is cleared and covered in
fresh gravel. There are plans to build an amphitheater, picnic pavilions,
more parking lots, a visitor's center, and a restaurant and to restore
Crystal Pier for boat tie-ups. But many people have other ideas.
Groups meet and argue about how the land should be used differently
and how it should be protected.

Meanwhile . . . they come on the Bay breeze, sailing in on downy
parachutes. They hitch rides in the mud balls on ducks' feet. They
arrive hooked on the feathers of gulls, on the socks of hikers, and on
the tires of bicycles and cars.

Seeds. Zillions of seeds.

Glossary

bacteria Kinds of microscopic living things. Some bacteria break down dead plant and animal material. Others live on the roots of plants and help them absorb the chemical nitrogen from the soil. Others act like algae and get energy from the sun. Still others cause diseases.

carrion Dead animal.

decomposers Living things that help in the decay and recycling of dead material. Bacteria, funguses, earthworms, and insects are all part of the recycling team.

dormant Of animals or plants, asleep or resting.

funguses Plantlike living things, such as mushrooms, that do not produce flowers, seeds, or their own food. Mold and mildew are also funguses.

larva An early stage in some creatures' lives when they look different from their parents.

maggot Wormlike fly larva.

mandibles Jaws used for chewing.

pioneer Plant or animal that is among the first to move into barren territory.

proboscis Long mouth part that an insect or other animal uses to reach into a food supply.

rhizome Runner or underground stem produced by some plants.

scat Animal droppings.

silt Sand and dirt carried by rivers from one place and deposited in another.

softshell crab A stage in a crab's growth. Again and again, a crab sheds (molts) its shell and grows a larger one. The crab is soft and helpless right after a molt and must hide until its new shell hardens.

underwater grasses Plants that grow in shallow water just offshore. They are not true grasses but submerged aquatic vegetation, or SAV. Grass beds slow down the movement of water and lessen the power of waves. Ducks eat seeds and leaves of the plants, and softshell crabs hide among them.

wave erosion The wearing away of land by the action of waves.